T0158936

That We All May Be One

A Biblical Perspective Regarding Race and the Gospel

Evangeline Henderson

WESTBOW
PRESS®
A DIVISION OF THOMAS NELSON
& ZONDERVAN

This book is a work of non-fiction. Unless otherwise noted, the author and the publisher make no explicit guarantees as to the accuracy of the information contained in this book and in some cases, names of people and places have been altered to protect their privacy.

Unless otherwise indicated, Scripture quotations in this publication are from the King James Version of the Bible.

GOD'S WORD is a copyrighted work of God's Word to the Nations Bible Society. Quotations are used by permission. Copyright 1995 by God's Word to the Nations Bible Society. All rights reserved.

Scripture taken from THE AMPLIFIED BIBLE, Old Testament copyright © 1965, 1987 by the Zondervan Corporation. The Amplified New Testament copyright © 1958, 1987 by The Lockman Foundation. Used by permission.

Scriptures quoted from *The Everyday Bible*, copyright © 1987 by Worthy Publishing, Fort Worth, Texas 76137. Used by permission.

WestBow Press books may be ordered through booksellers or by contacting:

WestBow Press
A Division of Thomas Nelson & Zondervan
1663 Liberty Drive
Bloomington, IN 47403
www.westbowpress.com
1 (866) 928-1240

ISBN: 978-1-5127-7354-5 (sc)
ISBN: 978-1-5127-7353-8 (e)

Library of Congress Control Number: 2017901421

Print information available on the last page.

WestBow Press rev. date: 2/22/2017

Contents

Dedication

First, I give all praise, honor, and glory to the Eternal Three for the vision that prompted the writing of this book. "Where there is no vision, the people perish" (Proverbs 29:18).

I dedicate this book to my parents, David N. Henderson (deceased) and Annie J. Henderson, and thank them for their wisdom, courage, love, and ceaseless instruction and guidance. Appreciation and recognition are to be accorded to them and countless others, living and deceased, for implementing the principles as instructed in Deuteronomy 6:6–9, 12 (GOD'S WORD):

> Take to heart these words that I give you today. Repeat them to your children. Talk about them when you're at home or away, when you lie down or get up. [Write them down, and] tie them around your wrist, and wear them as headbands as a reminder. Write them on the doorframes of your house and on your gates ... be careful that you don't forget the LORD.

May God help me and others to pass the torch of faith, courage, commitment, and pride on to the next generation!

Introduction

Neither pray I for these alone, but for them also
which shall believe on me through their word;
That they all may be one; as thou, Father, art in
me, and I in thee, that they also may be one in us:
that the world may believe that thou hast sent me.
—John 17:20–21

One of the recurring themes throughout the Bible is that of unity among the people of God. As Jesus prepared to face and endure the cruelty and agony of the cross, He did not forget His disciples or the church. His overwhelming desire and purpose was for His followers in every generation to be one as is the Trinity.

The prayer of Jesus in the above reference is of great importance. When He began His public ministry, He chose twelve men of various backgrounds and personalities to teach and train for ministry. All had potential, and all possessed natural talents and abilities that could be useful in the administration of their duties. Alone, these natural endowments were not sufficient. Before becoming ambassadors for Christ and the gospel, their characters had to be tested, their speech refined, their minds renewed, their preconceived ideas and opinions discarded, their hearts circumcised, and their prejudices and selfish ambitions crucified. Without a decided and necessary transformation, their concerted efforts in ministry would be futile.

The test of wills and conflict of personalities were evident in the interactions of the disciples with each other. Pride, jealousy, bigotry, and tradition were also strongholds that were constantly at work, threatening to destroy the unity Christ desired to see manifested in their lives. Throughout their three-year training period, Jesus patiently, through precept and example, taught them spiritual and practical lessons to aid them in acquiring spiritual maturity.

It was not until the day of Pentecost, when the outpouring of the Holy Spirit was manifested in His fullness and power, that the disciples understood what Jesus tried to reveal to them when He was with them. They had their Master's assurance that "the Comforter, which is the Holy Ghost, whom the Father will send in my name … shall teach you all things, and bring all things to your remembrance, whatsoever I have said unto you" (John 14:26). Filled with the Holy Spirit, the disciples were empowered to preach the gospel, accompanied by healings, signs, wonders, and miracles. Nevertheless, bigotry was an ever-present enemy against which spiritual warfare had to be waged.

Romans 12:2 says that believers are to "*be not conformed to this world*: but *be … transformed* by the renewing of your mind, that ye may prove what is that good, and acceptable, and perfect, will of God." We are not to imitate the ways and customs of the world. We are to be of one mind, have all things in common, and speak the same thing. Sadly, the body of Christ has adopted and adapted to the world's views, customs, traditions, and attitudes when it comes to biblical principles. While there is diversity in the body of Christ, there is also to be unity. If we are to live together for eternity in heaven, we must first learn to live together on this earth.

It was not an easy task getting twelve men to become one in unity and purpose. The challenge is even greater today, but it can be done. We have been given a new commandment by Jesus to love one another as He has loved us. It is this love for each other—unity—that will give unmistakable and convincing evidence to the world that Jesus is the Messiah, and that we are His disciples (John 13:34–35).

Chapter 1

What Is Truth?

Pilate therefore said unto him, Art thou a king
then? Jesus answered, Thou sayest that I am a king.
To this end was I born, and for this cause came I
into the world, that I should bear witness unto the
truth. Every one that is of the truth heareth my
voice. Pilate saith unto him, What is truth?
—John 18:37–38

My earliest recollections regarding race began with my parents.
They were well acquainted with the lessons—spoken and
unspoken—that segregation taught them. Both came from large
families and were born and reared during an era when Jim Crow
laws were the stronghold and signature of the South. Although
my parents often described to my siblings and me what life was
like living in a segregated society, it was my father who was
the most passionate on the subject. How I dreaded—as I now
recall with a wry smile—those discourses! It was difficult to
continually listen to incidents of injustice without being affected.
Some of the stories incensed me greatly. Others were sad and
depressing. There were, however, a few that were amusing, if not
downright funny, despite the somber and stressful conditions of
the time.

To speak truth, for several reasons I did not greatly care to have such unpleasant tales of racism rehearsed in my presence. First, as a child, I was not in a position to correct something that occurred long before I was born. When you're a black child living in America, you're told early on what is expected of you and how you will be perceived by others—especially whites. Unless you have parents who are strong role models to provide the spiritual as well as the emotional support needed to weather such opposition, you lose a sense of who you are—along with your purpose in life.

Second, I felt anger toward the offenders because they mistreated people of color because of their color and then invoked the law to justify their wicked behavior. Fear and anger would grip me to such an extent that I felt as if my very being was being consumed by an unseen force.

Third, in spite of the anger and anguish I felt, there was a part of me that really did not want to feel toward whites the same way that many of them felt toward us for something for which we were not responsible: the color of our skin. It was just as wrong to judge them for being white as they did us for being black.

The fourth reason for not wanting to hear about "the ghosts of racism past" was that I didn't know enough of the Word to fortify me in the way I needed at that time. I was taught that the Bible was God's holy Word and the book for successful living; that we were created in His image and likeness (Genesis 1:26–27); and that God so loved the world that He gave His only begotten Son, Jesus, to die for us—all of us—and free us from the bondage of sin so that we could have eternal life and go back with Him to live with Him in heaven (John 3:16; 14:1–3). While I knew and believed those words mentally and experientially, the true meaning of those words had yet to be revealed to me. Yes, I knew I was created in the image of God; the Bible said so. But my mind questioned, *If everything God made was good and His creation of humankind was very good, then why am I a color that is considered by many to be bad or unacceptable? If God is wise and intelligent, and I'm created in His image, I also possess similar attributes. If that is so, why am I constantly being reminded that I have to work twice as hard to prove that I am just as capable and intelligent as any white person?* What I read and heard contradicted what I *saw.* It did not make sense.

Inexplicably, I blamed God for being the color I was and for the stigma such a color produced. In my mind, I felt it was God's fault that I was experiencing discrimination. Then several years ago, the Holy Spirit impressed upon my mind something I had not considered nor have forgotten. Without warning, He spoke to me and said, "Evangeline, don't you think that God knew what color you'd be before you were born?" (See Jeremiah 1:4–5.) He made me realize how wrong and disrespectful I had been in blaming God for who and what I was. Color, to God, is insignificant. God *chose* to make me black. The fact that I did not comprehend the *why* behind His decision and reasoning did not alter His purpose in doing so.

James 1:5 says, "If any of you lack wisdom, *let him ask of God, that giveth to all men liberally, and upbraideth not; and it shall be given him"* (my emphasis). Amazingly, it never occurred to me to ask God to show me what I wanted or needed to know. I had been looking to my parents, the church, and others to supply the answers I needed. All were limited in the answers they could provide—answers that would not come in a day, a month, or a year. It would take time—years—before what I considered to be an enigma would become so simple. When the answers were revealed, not only were they realized in an unexpected manner, but they were right in front of me all the time. Their simplicity had been obscured by tradition, reasoning, and emotion.

Although I did not initially ask God for help, He sovereignly answered my unspoken cry for help and guidance. A pattern began to emerge, and I saw His leading and intervention in my circumstances. I did not understand then what I am sharing with you now. These incidents in my life were preparing me to receive further revelations that would radically change my perceptions concerning a lot of things, including racial issues. In time, I would come to understand that in order for me to know what truth was, I must first know Him who was and is the embodiment of truth: Jesus Christ.

What is truth? is an inquiry that has been answered by the authority of God's Word. In becoming acquainted with the One who is truth, I also came to know the reality of John 8:32: "And ye shall know the truth, and the truth shall make you free."

Chapter 2

A Lesson in Human Relations

> As we have therefore opportunity, let us do good
> unto all men, especially unto them who are of the
> household of faith.
>
> —Galatians 6:10

As we contemplate the subject of bigotry, we must not forget that it is not limited specifically to race. It encompasses gender, caste, class, and education.

Jesus was a master when it came to human relations. When He taught, preached, or healed, He attracted huge crowds of people wherever He went. Those drawn to Him represented every age group and station in life. His teachings appealed to the masses because they were simple and easy to understand. This was important because those in attendance were mostly uneducated. The object lessons He used from everyday life to enforce spiritual truths made an indelible impression upon the minds and hearts of His hearers. They were left to apply the principles they heard to their own lives and to make their own choices.

The nature and character of God had been misrepresented and misinterpreted by the spiritual leaders in Israel. These men prided themselves on their knowledge of the law of God and on being the children of Abraham, but they did not know the *spirit* of the law. Not only did they regard with disdain the Gentile nations around them, but they also took great pains to disassociate themselves from their own people—from those to whom they were to instruct and impart the sacred oracles.

Jesus's mission was to rectify the erroneous interpretations of the Scriptures concerning Himself and His ministry, and He was charged with revealing the true nature and character of God and His love for humankind (Luke 9:51–56).

The love and concern Jesus manifested in His daily intercourse with people was to be imitated by His followers then and in succeeding generations.

To impress this vital truth upon the hearts of the people, Jesus related a parable about the good Samaritan. Through this story is expressed the power of love. It is what brings people together, and it closes the door to hatred and division.

The Good Samaritan
Read Luke 10:25–37

The story begins with Jesus teaching the people. As He did so, "a certain lawyer [an expert in or professional teacher of the law of Moses] stood up, and tempted [tested] him, saying, Master, what shall I do to inherit eternal life?" (Luke 10:25). Have you ever noticed how Jesus was constantly interrupted when He was teaching? Either He initiated the interruption or someone or circumstances interrupted Him. The religious leaders and teachers especially liked to center the focus of their disputes with Jesus on certain aspects of the law. Their tactics were designed to ensnare Jesus and misconstrue His words in order that they might have something with which to accuse Him.

Jesus discerned the motive of the lawyer. Rather than permit Himself to be drawn into a religious debate, He had the lawyer answer his own question by posing one Himself: "What is written in the law? how readest thou?" (Luke 10:26). The lawyer responded, "Thou shalt love the Lord thy God with all thy heart, and with all thy soul, and with all thy strength, and with all thy mind; and thy neighbour as thyself" (Luke 10:27). The lawyer was correct in quoting what the law said; however, the question he asked Jesus pertaining to eternal life seemed to indicate that he was aware that something was missing. He may have honored God with his lips and outward show of piety, but that same devotion was not extended to others. Endeavoring to justify himself, the lawyer inquired, "And who is my neighbour?" (Luke 10:29). Jesus then related the parable of the good Samaritan.

He began the story by saying, "A certain man went down from Jerusalem to Jericho" (Luke 10:30). The road on which the man traveled was a perilous one. The traveler was violently attacked and robbed and left for dead in the road—in a spot where he would be visible to anyone traveling along the same road. A priest saw the victim but did not stop to help the injured man. He did not wish to be detained by anything or in this case, anyone. How do you see a human being lying in the road and feel no desire to stop and offer aid?

The next man to arrive on the scene was a Levite. Like the priest, he saw the man lying in the road. Unlike the priest, the Levite *came and looked on him*" (Luke 10:32). He assessed the man's condition, knew it was within his power to assist him, and *chose* not to help him! Did the image of that savagely beaten man ever leave the Levite's memory? We do not know. But do we not see these behaviors repeated in our day? People are victims of various forms of abuse or in trouble of some kind. There are witnesses to these incidents, but many refuse to get involved for fear of retaliation or are simply indifferent and do not want to be inconvenienced in any way. Like the priest and the Levite, they "pass by on the other side."

Aside from the selfishness of these two men in not wanting to help the victim, there was another reason for their cruelty: racism. They were unable to determine the victim's nationality. If the man was a Jew, depending on his social status, he still may have been ignored. If he was a foreigner, especially a Samaritan, he *definitely* would *not* have received aid!

The Jews and the Samaritans were not just enemies—they were *bitter* enemies and had no dealings with each other! (See John 4:5–9.) Jesus came to destroy the religious and cultural barriers that separated Jews and Gentiles "for to make in himself of twain one new man [humanity], so making peace" (Ephesians 2:14–15).

Thank God, the story doesn't end with the priest and the Levite! One more man traveled that same dangerous road. One more man saw what the other two men had seen: a wounded man in need of help. This man, however, was different ... *and* he was a *Samaritan*! When he saw the victim, "he had *compassion* on him" (Luke 10:33). Compassion was an attribute consistently manifested in Jesus's ministry—a love that was not limited "in word, neither in tongue; but in deed and in truth" (1 John 3:18).

The Samaritan not only stopped but tended to the victim's injuries, thus placing his own life in jeopardy. But it was a risk he was willing to take in order to ensure the man's safety from further harm.

The Samaritan placed the victim on his beast and transported him to an inn, where he was carefully watched during the night. The next morning, as the Samaritan prepared to leave, he placed the man in the custody of the innkeeper. He gave the innkeeper money for the man's care and promised reimbursement upon his return, if further expenses were incurred.

We are not told how long the stranger stayed at the inn until he was well enough to leave. Nor are we told whether the injured man was informed of the deed of his benefactor. Hopefully, he was appreciative for the kindness shown to him by a stranger.

The story now concluded, Jesus asked, "Which now of these three, thinkest thou, was neighbour unto him that fell among the thieves?" (Luke 10:36). Instead of acknowledging the Samaritan by name, the tone of the lawyer's response still manifested the prevailing attitude of society and his own bigotry: "*He* that shewed mercy on him" (Luke 10:37). Jesus then gives him a directive: *"Go, and do thou likewise"* (Luke 10:37). Our neighbor is *anyone* in need of our compassion. If we say that we love God, our actions will mirror that of the good Samaritan, who is representative of Christ.

Jesus's response to the lawyer should evoke from each one of us a personal inquiry: *Which of these three men am I?*

Chapter 3

Can I Get a Witness? (Part 1): A Whale of a Lesson

In the mouth of two or three witnesses shall every word be established.

—2 Corinthians 13:1

The Bible should be our primary reference in securing answers that lay the proper foundation and provide the correct understanding of God's will and purpose for the salvation of humanity. As referenced above, two or three witnesses are confirmation that something is valid. Confirmation is not merely applicable in terms of persons but also Scriptures. If at least two or three Scriptures can be found to support understanding and clarification on a given subject, then we are assured that it is Bible truth.

For the purpose of this discourse, we will use the life experiences of two men: one from the Old Testament and one from the New Testament. One man was a prophet, the other an apostle. Both were called by God to preach the gospel to a specific group of people. Both had the same problem: bigotry. Each man's experience revealed his faults and failures and the struggle to overcome national pride. Each man's story is our story. More amazing than God's grace are the methods God employs to reveal to His servants His mercy and salvation to all humankind, even when the chosen vessel is less than cooperative!

Read the Book of Jonah.

In Jonah 1:1, 2, we see that "the word of the LORD came unto Jonah" to "go to Nineveh." He was being sent to pronounce judgment on the city because of the wickedness of its inhabitants. Jonah, however, did not want to go, and "rose up to flee unto Tarshish from the presence of the LORD" (Jonah 1:3). Surely he knew the truth of the adage, "You can run, but you can't hide," especially from God. Interestingly, God made no attempt to stop Jonah's flight. He watched Jonah flee to Tarshish, pay his fare, go down into the ship, get comfortable, and fall fast asleep. He watched the ship pull out of the port and travel far into the sea. Then God showed up and introduced Himself in a very dramatic way!

> But the LORD sent out a great wind into the sea,
> and there was a mighty tempest in the sea, so that
> the ship was like to be broken (Jonah 1:4).

It is amazing that Jonah was able to sleep amid the violence of the storm. The only reason Jonah was aware of the danger the ship and its passengers were in was because the captain of the ship had to awaken him and tell him to pray (Jonah 1:5–6)! A worldly person should not have to tell a believer what to do, especially in a crisis situation!

The ship was carrying men of various nationalities, backgrounds, and religions. They sensed that someone on the ship was responsible for the trouble they were experiencing. They decided to cast lots in order to identify the culprit. The lot fell on Jonah! When you disobey God, God has a way of exposing you and using sinners and unbelievers to do so! Jonah acknowledged that he was a Hebrew, and feared "the LORD, the God of heaven, which hath made the sea and the dry land"

(Jonah 1:9). He took responsibility for his actions and requested that he be cast overboard so that no innocent persons would needlessly perish. The men tried their best to get the ship to land without resorting to such drastic action, but they finally had no choice but to do as Jonah suggested. Once Jonah hit the water, "the sea ceased from her raging. Then the men feared the LORD exceedingly, and offered a sacrifice unto the LORD, and made vows" (Jonah 1:15–16).

Jonah not only imperiled the lives of innocent people but also his own life. He would surely have drowned had God not "prepared a great fish to swallow up Jonah" (Jonah 1:17). That was followed by three days and three nights of reflection inside the fish, after which he "prayed unto the LORD his God out of the fish's belly" (Jonah 2:1). He acknowledged his sin and repented of his disobedience. His fate would have been the same as the Ninevites were it not for God's intervention on his behalf. Weren't the people of Nineveh to be given what Jonah had received but did not deserve: a second chance?

When the second call came for Jonah to go to Nineveh, he obeyed. Upon his arrival, he began to proclaim the message of judgment against the city. While Jonah was grateful that *his* life had been spared, he still was not willing that Nineveh should be accorded the same courtesy. How soon he had forgotten his own brush with death; his confession of sin and repentance; his heartfelt prayer for forgiveness and remembrance of God's mercy; and his miraculous deliverance from the belly of the whale. After preaching the message given to him by God, he waited to witness its fulfillment. To his dismay, the people of Nineveh heeded the warning and repented. Even the animals were included (Jonah 3:7–8). The actions of the Ninevites showed that they believed God (Jonah 3:5). The judgments pronounced upon the city and its inhabitants of that generation were stayed. (Eventually, the Ninevites returned to their former ways. The judgments of God, which previously had been held in check, were released, and the city and its residents were destroyed.)

Our last glimpse of Jonah portrays a man full of pride, whine, and a stubborn will. Displeased that the impending judgment did not occur, Jonah pleaded with God to take his life. In response, God desired to show Jonah his selfishness and wrong attitude. Using a plant as an object lesson, God reproved Jonah for having pity on a plant rather than on 120,000 people in a city. God provided the plant because of His mercy and love. It was a blessing that Jonah received and enjoyed. He had no control over it and had no right to be angry when it was removed. God permitted the demise of the plant at His discretion, and it was not for Jonah to question His decision to do so.

When Jonah balked at going to Nineveh and disobeyed God, God could have destroyed him on the spot. He did not. He let Jonah's foolishness run its course and then intervened. Jonah repented of his disobedience but only after he nearly lost his life. The Ninevites, on the other hand, had a history of violence and bloodshed. When the Ninevites heard the message and its pronouncement of doom, *they repented immediately*! God honored their repentance by sparing their lives as He had spared the life of Jonah.

Here's a question for us to ponder: *When truth is presented to us and we are shown that we are wrong—when it becomes a matter of repentance and obedience, is our response like that of Jonah or the people of Nineveh?*

Chapter 4

Can I Get a Witness? (Part 2): Two Men plus Two Visions Equal One Purpose

> For ye are all the children of God by faith in Christ Jesus.
>
> —Galatians 3:26

Read Acts 10–11.

We've seen an example of God dealing with a stubborn Old Testament prophet to bring the message of salvation to the inhabitants of a wicked city. Now let us turn our attention to an example from the New Testament.

Cornelius, a Roman army officer in the Italian regiment, lived in Caesarea. He was well-respected and loved—a good man with a kind heart and good intentions. He had a knowledge of God and was acting on that knowledge to the best of his ability. God knew Cornelius's heart, knew that he was seeking truth. All he needed was someone to fill in the missing pieces by leading him to a saving knowledge of Jesus Christ. God knew just the man for the job: Peter. That's right, Peter, the one who was the most outspoken and self-confident of the twelve disciples, who had been privileged to be taught and trained by Jesus. The one who emphatically declared that he would go with Jesus to prison and to death, then forsook Him and fled (as did all of the disciples)!

The one who, along with James and John, was found sleeping when Jesus warned him to watch and pray in the garden of Gethsemane. The one (the *only* one) who ventured out of the boat during a violent storm and walked on water—then took his eyes off of Jesus and nearly drowned! He was the one who steadfastly proclaimed that he would *never* deny Jesus, then denied him three times—complete with cursing and swearing! He wept bitterly, and sincerely repented of his shameful behavior. Yes, this same Peter was specifically selected for this important assignment.

Why Peter? One reason may be that God knew Peter's heart. He was well aware of the defects in Peter's character, but He also knew what it would take to bring those defects to light where they would have to be confronted and rectified.

But there was another reason why Peter was chosen. Before Jesus ascended to heaven, He told His disciples to wait in Jerusalem—that they were to "be baptized with the Holy Ghost" (Acts 1:5) and receive power that would enable them to be witnesses for Him. Peter and the other disciples prepared themselves for this event through prayer and supplication. When the day of Pentecost arrived, the endowment of power promised was realized. During this time, Jews from every nation were in Jerusalem and heard the gospel preached in their own specific language and dialect. As a result, three thousand souls were added to the church (Acts 2:5-11, 41). But God also desired non-Jewish people to hear the message of salvation. It is one thing to preach to thousands of people where personal one-to-one contact is limited or nonexistent *and* those hearing the message are all of the same faith and/or nationality. It is another thing to witness to someone of another race and culture that you have been taught and trained to believe is inferior to you, and who is considered to be your enemy. It was this situation into which Peter was thrust. Just as prayer prepared the disciples to receive the outpouring of the Holy Spirit on the day of Pentecost, so prayer would be essential in preparing Cornelius and Peter to understand, receive, and accept their respective visions and revelations ... and each other.

One day, while Cornelius was praying, he had a vision and saw an angel coming in to him. The angel told him that God had noticed his deeds, and that a man named Simon, surnamed Peter, would provide further insight and instruction. He was to send for Peter and informed as to where he could be found. Cornelius obeyed. Two of his household servants and a devout soldier were sent to Joppa to summon Peter.

The next day, Peter, unaware of what was about to occur, was waiting for lunch to be served. As the meal was being prepared, "Peter went up upon the housetop to pray" (Acts 10:9) and subsequently fell into a trance and had a vision. He "saw heaven opened, and a certain vessel descending unto him, as it had been a great sheet knit at the four corners, and let down to the earth" (Acts 10:11). The sheet contained all kinds of four-footed animals, reptiles, and birds. Peter was commanded to kill and eat them. He refused, saying he had never eaten anything common or unclean. God told him that *what He had cleansed was not to be called common or unclean*. This happened three times. Then the sheet was received again into heaven and the vision ended. Initially, Peter was perplexed as to the meaning of the vision. But then the Holy Spirit spoke to Peter, telling him that he was being sought by three men, and that he was to go with them without hesitation because He had sent them.

Don't you love how personal God is? Don't you love how God brings people together and makes things happen in ways we never could have imagined? I once heard Pastor John Hagee say during one of his sermons several years ago that when God tells you to do something and you understand it and do it, that's obedience. When God tells you to do something and you *don't* understand it, but do it anyway, that's *faith*. Both men took a risk in doing something that went against the social norm. Because they exercised faith by obeying God, they and the church received a tremendous blessing.

Imagine Peter's emotions and the thoughts that filled his mind as he and the three men set out on the return trip to Caesarea. Knowing how news travels quickly and the uproar such a visit would be sure to excite, "certain brethren from Joppa accompanied him [Peter]" as witnesses on this eventful journey (Acts 10:23). The wisdom of his actions would later be confirmed when Peter found himself in the position of having to defend his actions (Acts 11:1–18).

Upon arriving at the home of Cornelius, they "found many that were come together" (Acts 10:27). Cornelius related his experience to Peter, ending with "Now therefore are we all here present before God, to hear all things that are commanded thee of God" (Acts 10:33). With such receptivity before him, Peter exclaimed, *"Of a truth I perceive that God is no respecter of persons: But in every nation he that feareth him, and worketh righteousness, is accepted with him"* (Acts 10:34–35). Peter then began to preach the gospel of Jesus Christ. While he was speaking, "the Holy Ghost fell on all them which heard the word. For they [those that came with Peter] heard them speak with tongues, and magnify God" (Acts 10:44, 46). Proof of God's acceptance of the Gentiles was given through the baptism of the Holy Spirit with the evidence of speaking in other tongues. It was the same experience as that of the one hundred twenty disciples on the day of Pentecost (Acts 2:1–4; 10:45). After receiving the baptism of the Holy Spirit, Cornelius and those present with him received water baptism, being "baptized in the name of the Lord" (Acts 10:47–48). This is the experience of everyone who is born again.

If Peter had not had these two experiences (being *born* of the Spirit and then *filled* with the Spirit)—if he had not been led to pray; if he had not had the vision; if the Holy Spirit had not told him to go with the three men whom Cornelius had sent— Peter would not have set his foot anywhere *near* Cornelius's house, let alone *in* it! Peter even said as much to Cornelius: "Ye know how that it is an unlawful thing for a man that is a Jew to keep company, or come unto one of another nation; but *God hath shewed me that I should not call any man common or unclean"* (Acts 10:28).

Peter realized that the vision he received was a revelation of God's will to include the Gentiles in the plan of salvation, but at times, he lapsed into moments of weakness. In one instance, the apostle Paul had to publicly rebuke Peter for his hypocrisy regarding his treatment of the Gentiles while at Antioch. (See Galatians 2:11–21.)

Let's not be too harsh in our judgment of Peter. How many of us have been segregated via civil laws and/or through self-imposed actions to the extent that when circumstances necessitate a change in custom, we find ourselves feeling uncomfortable, traumatized, or unable to comply accordingly? How many parents or others in authority by precept and/or example have reinforced upon impressionable minds "how that it is an unlawful thing to keep company or come unto one of another nation" with anyone other than their own race? How many of us, verbally or silently, thought of others as "common or unclean"?

Those of us who desire to be continually filled with and led by the Holy Spirit will find that His promptings will lead us to disregard and discard long-held cherished customs and traditions. It will require us to step out of our comfort zone and into the unknown. How many of us are ready and willing to relinquish the familiar and ordinary and experience the exciting realm of the supernatural? It will happen for those who believe God and the promises given as to the signs and wonders that will follow the believers. It will also take courage and determination to be obedient in the face of opposition from without (the world) and within (the church and ourselves). There is an adage that says that every obstacle introduces a person to himself. Jonah and Peter had to learn this lesson, and so must we. Tough tests and hard times reveal the true character of a person. Each victory prepares us for the next test. Obedience increases spiritual growth and sensitivity to the Holy Spirit and His leading.

Jonah and Peter were chosen to do something that, in the natural, neither would have initiated on his own. God used a whale to stop a disobedient prophet from running from his call and warn a wicked city of impending judgment. He used a vision to lead Peter to minister in the home of a Gentile.

What will God use to get *your* attention and get *you* out of *your* comfort zone so that *you* can be used by Him to "open the blind eyes, to bring out the prisoners from the prison, and them that sit in darkness out of the prison house" (Isaiah 42:7)?

Jonah and Peter had much in common, and I was about to join their company. Little did I know that God had chosen me for two unusual assignments—and He would use two unusual men to introduce me to myself!

Chapter 5

A Tale of Two Men (Part 1): The Death of a Stranger

On Tuesday, March 28, 2000, an intense spirit of prayer came upon me. I spent the entire day praying in the Spirit (praying in tongues), despite suffering from a migraine headache, which began the previous afternoon. That evening, as my headache subsided, I was reading the local newspaper. I came across the obituary section and saw a photograph of a young man that nearly took my breath away.

I did not know the deceased; he was a stranger to me. He grew up in a small town, twenty to thirty minutes from where I lived, but had moved away from the area. According to the death announcement, he had lived in New York and abroad before residing in a major city on the West Coast. While on vacation, he died while swimming. While specific details surrounding his death were somewhat shrouded in mystery, it was obvious that his demise was sudden and tragic. He was three days shy of celebrating what would have been his thirty-sixth birthday.

He was quite handsome. With his looks, he could have been a model instead of working in the music industry, which he obviously loved. But there was something about his eyes that held me spellbound—a look of sadness and longing in them. It was what I saw in his eyes, what I could not explain or describe, that shook me to the core of my being. The image stayed with me the remainder of the evening and haunted me through a restless night. With the dawning of a new day came an urgency and an intense determination from deep within my spirit—something that rarely manifested itself, especially when it involved strangers. To this day, I cannot tell you why, but for some reason, I had to see him. I would have no peace until I did.

The funeral was scheduled for that Friday morning. On Wednesday, I called the funeral home to inquire when the remains would be available for viewing. After answering my question, the gentleman with whom I spoke asked me a question I had not anticipated.

"Are you a member of the family?"

"Oh, uh … no. I don't know this young man. I just saw his picture in the obituary section, you know, and uh, it just left me with a really odd feeling. And I just felt the need to see him."

Silence.

"Well, thank you for your time. You have a nice day!"

I quickly hung up the telephone, berating myself profusely for doing something so asinine. My face was still warm from embarrassment over what I had just done. Then the devil put in his two cents' worth to make my discomfiture complete.

Girl, what on earth were you thinking, calling down to that funeral home? You don't know this guy. Why do you want to see him? Even you can't answer that. That man must have thought you were a nut 'cause you sounded like one! You need to leave it alone!

But I can't leave it alone, I argued. *The Holy Spirit won't let me! I don't know why I need to see him. I just do.*

Back and forth it went, the devil and the thoughts in my head, the rest of the day until by late afternoon, I was thoroughly exhausted. I could not believe the battle I was having with myself. Finally, in desperation, I cried out, "Father, I can't take this! I don't know what's going on, why this guy's death is affecting me like this, or why I need to see him. None of this makes any sense to me. I'm not bothering with this anymore. Please, just take it from me!" The Father, however, was not willing to let me off the hook until I accomplished what He purposed for me to do in this situation.

Thursday morning, the battle resumed. For my part, it was an effort in futility. I finally surrendered to the Father's will. I prayed, asking Father for wisdom and guidance in preparing a letter to the family as prompted by the Holy Spirit; to relate to them His message of love, hope, and comfort. The letter was enclosed in a personalized sympathy card. It was my intention to go to the funeral home prior to the wake, leave the card with a staff member, and return home.

Unforeseeable circumstances precluded me from fulfilling my original plan. By the time I arrived at the funeral home, it was almost 6:30 p.m. My mind was racing, as was my heart, as I made my way through the evening rush hour traffic. Despite the delay in the time of my arrival, I still cherished the thought and hope of a rapid entry, drop off, and getaway. The Holy Spirit, however, had other ideas!

Once inside, I made my way down the long, carpeted corridor. It was huge, spacious, and immaculate, with high ceilings and chandelier light fixtures. The only thing stronger than the silence that filled the hallway was the anointing that had been upon me all day. It seemed to increase in intensity after my arrival.

A tall, elderly gentleman, stately in his bearing with salt and pepper hair, appeared near the end of the corridor near the stairs leading to the lower level. As I approached him, he spoke.

"May I help you?" he asked. He seemed polite and friendly enough. His manner eased my fears somewhat. I had come dressed appropriately for the occasion (suit, heels, hat, and coat), even though I had planned to stay only a New York minute. You know what they say about first impressions.

"Yes, sir. Good evening. My name is Evangeline Henderson, and I wanted to leave a card for the K__ family. May I leave it with you to give to them?" I handed him the envelope. He took it and looked at it thoughtfully.

"Certainly," he replied.

I thanked him, then turned around and started to retrace my steps. *Well, that was easier than I thought*, I mused. Wrong. About three or four steps into my retreat, he called to me.

"Miss?" I stopped and turned to face him.

"Sir?"

"Would you like to give this to the family yourself?"

No, not really, I wanted to say. I was momentarily caught off guard. All my thoughts and efforts had centered on getting in and getting out. It never occurred to me that I would find myself in this position. Now what? I explained that I did not know the deceased or the family but was impressed to leave a card for the family. I did not want to intrude. I was hoping that my explanation would cause him to change his mind regarding his inquiry. His next words were thoughtful, but somewhat insistent.

"I think you should give this to the family. I'm sure they would appreciate it."

"Oh, okay," I said rather reluctantly. So much for a quick escape. I continued, "How do I get to the chapel?"

After being given the directions, he returned the envelope I'd given him moments earlier. I thanked him and proceeded downstairs. With each step, my mind was frantically rehearsing what I would say, if my voice ever showed up! The devil sure did, and picked up where he'd left off twenty-four hours before with his tormenting accusations.

See, I told you! You should have left it alone! Now what are you going to do? What are these white folks going to think when they see you walk through that door? They're going to put you out! You got no business being here. They don't know you. What are you going to say to these folks? You'll probably be the only black in there. How's that going to make you feel?

I could say nothing in my defense. Part of me wanted to retreat and go home, but pride, duty, and the anointing prevented me from doing so. No matter how much trouble I was having with my head, my feet kept walking toward the chapel. I would see this through, no matter what happened.

Moments later, I arrived at the door leading into the chapel. Taking a deep breath, I turned the doorknob and walked in. A few people had already arrived to pay their respects. Looking toward the front of the chapel, I saw the beautiful wood-carved casket containing the deceased.

As I took in my surroundings, I was acutely aware that the devil had been right about one thing: I *was* the only person of color in the room. If my presence was displeasing, annoying, or otherwise unwelcome, it was not expressed verbally. In fact, I was virtually ignored. While I managed to maintain a calm, cool exterior, my face was growing warmer by the minute. A ragged mini-line had formed, and to this I joined myself. One by one, individuals and couples expressed their condolences to an elderly woman (one of the grandmothers, I suspected) and an attractive young woman with short, dark brown hair, perhaps in her late twenties or early thirties, standing beside her. The deceased had only one sibling, a sister, according to the death announcement. I assumed this was she. The grandmother, a short, medium build woman, who appeared to be gracious and gentle, spoke quietly and effortlessly, acknowledging with gratitude those who shared her loss. She seemed quite composed and dignified, reminiscent in character and bearing of the traditional expectation of most Southern matriarchs in the face of crisis or tragedy. In contrast, her granddaughter said little to nothing, except to manage an occasional smile. A white handkerchief or Kleenex tissue never seemed to leave her hand as her silent tears fell continually from her eyes. At times, she seemed to stare at the floor, then into space, and then at nothing.

The brief line continued to move until I found myself only a few feet away from them. There was a momentary pause as I motioned to a couple to my right to go ahead of me. They started to go forward when, for some strange reason, they abruptly stopped. In the midst of a somewhat awkward silence, I literally felt an unseen hand nudge me toward the grandmother until I was standing right in front of her! The next thing I knew, I heard myself speaking. The grandmother smiled as I introduced myself, told her how and why I came to be there, conveyed my sympathy to her and the family, and then gave her the card and note. As I talked, I observed, out of the corner of my eye, the young woman watching me with keen interest.

When I finished speaking, to my surprise, the grandmother said, "Let me show you what my grandson wrote. He was a songwriter." She then produced a funeral program, which included the lyrics to a song he had co-written as well as some personal thoughts from his private journal. Then, quite unexpectedly, she asked, "Would you like a program?" I had not expected any generosity, especially since I was not a known acquaintance. I graciously replied, "Yes, I would. Thank you." She handed me a funeral program, then asked me to sign the register at the opposite end of the chapel. I asked for permission to view the body. Nodding her assent, she thanked me for coming.

After signing the register, I went to the casket and stood there for a few moments, gazing at the young man I only knew from a photograph in the newspaper. I had wanted—needed—to see him. My desire had been realized, and now here he was before me. It was a surreal moment. He was casually dressed in a black turtleneck top; dark pants, I believe; a medium tan-colored leather jacket; and a turquoise oval-shaped ring on his right pinky finger.

I know it sounds absurd, but it felt strange, almost uncomfortable, for me to be viewing the remains of a white person in a casket after seeing nothing but black faces and bodies all of my life. Death is no respecter of persons. Yet, when death comes, why are we? The young man before me wasn't just some white guy who died suddenly and tragically. He was a human being worthy of being loved and mourned. He was a son, a brother, an uncle, a cousin, a grandson, a neighbor, a classmate, a friend. All who knew him loved and lost someone who meant something special to them personally. For each person, the level of grief was different. It shouldn't have mattered that he was white. However, in the back of my mind, I couldn't help wondering what this guy would have thought, said, felt, or done if he could have opened his eyes and seen me standing there looking at him.

The voices in the background brought me back from my reverie and to my senses. I came to fulfill a mission; my duty was done. It was time to go. I walked to the back of the chapel and prepared to leave. As I walked to the door leading to the outer court, I happened to glance to my left. I caught the eye of the sister, whose tears seemed to have temporarily abated to give me a curious, wondering smile, the keen interest still evident in her eyes. I smiled in return, then walked out of the chapel. Although no words were ever spoken between us, it was as though our smiles acknowledged a sort of mutual respect for one another. Maybe that's all that was needed. Sometimes words get in the way.

The older gentleman I'd met earlier was still standing where I'd left him. When I reached the top of the stairs, I told him to have a good evening. He thanked me. Finally, I reached the front entrance and stepped out into the breezy March evening. Once outside, the anointing, which had rested so heavily upon me all day, immediately lifted, and I was at peace.

A stranger's untimely death revealed defects in my character that needed to be overcome. It summoned strength and boldness to rise up and confront mindsets and fears, invisible enemies that beset and endeavor to impede us from fulfilling God's will in our lives.

This experience prepared me to accept another challenge even greater than what I'd already encountered. For the second time, it would be another white man. Once again, the battle with insecurities, doubts, fears, and unanswered questions would be renewed with greater intensity. This time, however, two things would be different: 1) This man would be *very* much alive, and 2) Although I did not know him personally nor had we ever met, he would definitely be no stranger!

Chapter 6

A Tale of Two Men (Part 2): A Startling Revelation

> But the Lord said unto him [Ananias], Go thy way:
> for he is a chosen vessel unto me, to bear my name
> before the Gentiles, and kings, and the children
> of Israel: For I will shew him how great things he
> must suffer for my name's sake.
>
> —Acts 9:15–16

In Acts 9, we read about Saul of Tarsus, who later became known as the apostle Paul, and his life-changing conversion experience. While traveling to Damascus for the purpose of arresting men and women who were followers of Jesus Christ, Saul was literally knocked off of his high horse by a blinding glory of light. He heard a voice call him by name and ask him why he was persecuting Him. When Saul inquired as to the identity of the Speaker, Jesus let him know that it was He against whom Saul was fighting. Saul then asked what he should do. He was told to go into the city of Damascus and wait for further instructions.

A disciple in Damascus named Ananias received a vision from Jesus regarding Saul and a message relating His will and purpose for Saul's life. Ananias was to go and lay hands on Saul that his sight might be restored and he would be filled with the Holy Spirit. As hands were laid upon Saul, the Scripture says,

"And immediately there fell from his eyes as it had been scales: and he received sight forthwith, and arose, and was baptized" (Acts 9:18).

Like Saul, I had an encounter with the Lord of a different nature. I received a revelation that continued over a period of almost two weeks concerning the issue of race and its relation to the gospel. The following is an account of my "Damascus road" experience.

Trouble had been brewing after it was announced by our local county Board of Supervisors to recognize the month of April as Confederate History and Heritage Month. The decision sparked public outrage and racial tensions in our area, particularly in the black community. To make matters worse, a prominent black minister, who objected to the proposal, was denied an opportunity to speak at the public hearing regarding the decision. Incensed, the minister expressed his displeasure by staging a boycott or "blackout" of two area shopping malls to be held on Saturday, April 1, 2000. The controversy caught the attention of another prominent leader. A well-known white supremacist made the decision to counter the minister's protest on the same day. The stage was being set for a racial showdown.

The only way that a serious confrontation could be avoided was through the avenue of prayer. As a result of prevailing prayer, David Duke's visit to Richmond lasted all of twenty minutes. For the business owners at both malls (white and minorities), significant financial losses were incurred. Had the minister and the members of his congregation sought the Lord through intercessory prayer rather than succumbing to the course of action taken, the outcome would have been far different.

The controversy gradually subsided, and things returned to normal. If I thought the matter was over, I was about to discover that it was not over for me.

During the morning hours of April 1, I was in the privacy of my bedroom praying in the Spirit. The Holy Spirit spoke to me and told me to prepare a letter the following day (Sunday) to be mailed to the minister. He gave me specific thoughts and Scriptures to be included in the correspondence. The next day, the letter was prepared and mailed on Monday, April 3.

When one speaks in an unknown tongue, the Bible says that he (that is, the person doing the speaking) speaks mysteries (1 Corinthians 14:2). The Everyday Bible states that "he is speaking secret things through the Spirit." The apostle Paul tells us that we are to pray that we may interpret what is being spoken in an unknown tongue (1 Corinthians 14:13). There was no doubt in my mind that what the Holy Spirit revealed to me was the interpretation or essence of my prayers that Saturday morning as well as what I had been praying during the course of the week.

During the preparation of the letter, I had some trepidation as to whether or not I would receive a response and/or the type of response the letter would generate. Secretly, I cherished the thought and hope that the minister would reply so that I could gauge his receptivity to the communication.

I did receive a reply ... but not from the minister. The confirmation came from an unexpected source. On Tuesday, April 4, an editorial appeared in our local newspaper concerning the boycott. To my utter astonishment, some of the views and statements expressed by the editor echoed the sentiments I had written to the minister! The Father had graciously granted the desire of my heart and given me the encouragement I needed. The manner in which He chose to answer was such that it was unbiased and my emotions were protected. While a part of me, at times, still wonders what the minister thought of the letter, it is enough that God responded in the manner that He deemed best.

The letter to the minister was only part of my assignment. There was more to come. Later that night, I received a startling revelation.

"Are You Kidding Me?"

After saying my prayers, I practically fell into bed. I was mentally and emotionally exhausted from the events of the week, and praying in tongues all day. How I looked forward to a good night's sleep. But sleep was the last thing my spirit man wanted to do! As I lay in bed in the darkened room, except for the reflection of light from the street lamp in our front yard peering through the closed blinds, it soon grew quiet. A few moments later, I found myself praying in tongues again. All of a sudden, the most incredible thing came out of my mouth! It was as if someone else was speaking through me, and I was merely listening to what was being said. I heard myself quote Acts 9:1–16 *verbatim*! When I finished, *immediately* David Duke's face flashed in front of me. In that instant, I knew what the Spirit of God was saying to me. I could hardly believe what my mouth said and my ears heard! Before I realized what I was doing, I bolted to an upright position and said, half aloud, "Are You kidding me?" *No way*, I thought. *That can't be right. Him?* However, my attitude toward David Duke began to change.

All that I had seen, heard, or read about this former Klansman had been negative. I, like countless others, had judged him by what my eyes saw and what my ears heard (Isaiah 11:3). In the coming weeks and months ahead, I would learn the wisdom of the admonition given in the Word about the sin of judging people. I would find myself confessing and repenting of this particular sin in regard to him. For the first time, I began to really understand what Father desires to do in bringing us together as one humanity, and what He desired to do in the life of this man. The Holy Spirit also brought to my remembrance Duke's political bid several years ago to become governor of Louisiana. His plans were thwarted when he was defeated. Had he won, much damage would have been done as a result of his influence. As of this writing, Mr. Duke is again seeking to represent the state of Louisiana, but in a different capacity.

In July, 2016, he announced his candidacy by registering for Louisiana's US Senate race. David Duke was and is a hated man, but God sees in him a man He can use to further His kingdom. Whether Mr. Duke fills his place in the plan of God will depend upon his full surrender to and cooperation with Him.

From "Speaking Secrets" to Keeping a Secret

When I first received this revelation, it was a struggle resisting the temptation to share it with someone. I knew the danger in revealing what God had shown me before He gave me permission to do so. I had to be careful. I did, in limited, vague fashion, confide in a spiritual family friend, but no one else. Like Mary, I had to keep all these things and ponder them in my heart (Luke 2:19).

In the days that followed, I wondered why the Father chose to reveal this "secret" to me. Surely there must have been some others before me who may have been privileged with this revelation. What was I to do with this information besides pray concerning its fulfillment? It wasn't long before the answer came. The command from the Lord was clear: *I was to write a letter to David Duke.* It wasn't something that the Holy Spirit actually *said*, but more or less an inward witness, a knowing in my spirit that this was what I was to do. *Dear Lord*, I thought, *I can't do that!* I was literally afraid to act on it. Images from past history regarding the Klan flooded my mind: lynchings ... bombings ... cross burnings ... angry white mobs. My thoughts then turned to my family. They knew nothing of the revelation or the command from the Lord that I had received. Uncertain of what might occur, I worried that my life as well as the lives of my family would be imperiled. If violence landed on our doorstep, they would have no knowledge or understanding of what precipitated the provocation. I knew what I needed to do, but fear kept me from doing it.

The Father had given me the assurance of His favor and protection through a specific word: "Be not afraid, but speak, and hold not thy peace: For I am with thee, and no man shall set on thee to hurt thee" (Acts 18:9–10). That should have allayed my fears and encouraged me to commence my task. Unfortunately, my head and emotions got in the way. I knew I was the Father's choice to do this, but I did not want to be. I wanted Him to choose someone else, but He didn't. So for nearly three months, I did nothing. Although the burden would wane a little at times, it did not completely go away.

By this time, I had had the baptism of the Holy Spirit for almost eight years. I had enough experiences to know and understand spiritual things. Even though I was eight years along regarding the ways and the move of the Spirit, I still found myself being reluctant to move in certain areas as prompted by the Spirit. I thank the Lord for His mercy toward and patience with me during this time. As the late Kenneth E. Hagin used to say, "God will put up with a little unbelief in you, if you don't know any better. But when you know better, you can't get by with it." I knew better. I also knew that I was on the verge of dangerously grieving the Holy Spirit. By allowing myself to be consumed with fear, preventing me from performing a known act of duty, I was operating in unbelief. I had God's word that I would not be harmed. To continue to be disobedient would not only bring judgment on Mr. Duke, if he continued to pursue his course of action, but also on me for failing to give him God's message of warning and reproof. Refusing to obey also brought misery. The prompting of the Holy Spirit and call to duty finally brought me to my knees as well as to my senses.

Having made the decision to be obedient, I then began to earnestly inquire of the Lord as to how to go about preparing the correspondence to Mr. Duke. I really didn't know anything about him, let alone how to contact him. The Holy Spirit showed me how to access the information I needed, and my research began. I read various articles and excerpts from a book he had written to get an idea of his character and way of thinking. Many of his writings, comments, or actions appalled me or provoked me to absolute rage! On the other hand, I had to admit that there were some general statements he made that were factual and true. I also learned some things about him of which I was not previously aware.

Satan on Assignment

It was my assumption (and perhaps that of others as well) that David Duke had always been a white supremacist. To my surprise, that was *not* true. In his book entitled *My Awakening: A Path to Racial Understanding*, he makes mention of the fact that in his early years, he sympathized with the plight of blacks in this country. He had watched with interest the Civil Rights Movement as blacks, under the leadership of the Rev. Dr. Martin Luther King, Jr., used nonviolent methods in demanding equal rights, justice, and opportunities for themselves and other minorities. His family had a black housekeeper named Pinky, whose authority he had to respect and obey as he would that of his own parents. He had even learned how to be opinionated from her! When she died, they attended her funeral. So what, you may ask, caused him to change his attitude and course of life? Believe it or not, a class assignment!

One of his teachers gave the class an assignment where the students were to select a topic or issue of interest and take the opposite point of view. Mr. Duke's interest was in the Civil Rights Movement. In taking the opposing view, he had to find information to support it. His efforts resulted in perplexity and frustration when he could not find what he needed in the public library or through other conventional resources. Finally, a librarian apprised him of a discreet location where he could obtain the information he needed. Among the books he read was one entitled *Race and Reason*. This book, primarily, changed the course of his life, and greatly influenced his thinking and passion regarding the issue of race.

When I read this, I could not help but feel that Satan was

the instigator behind the whole thing. Satan knew and saw the attributes that God wanted to use for a noble cause and ran interference to use those same attributes for his own sinister designs. Satan has ever been the thief who comes to steal, kill, and destroy (John 10:10). He actuated the teacher to unwittingly give a class assignment that would cause David Duke's impressionable mind to be influenced to the degree that he would embrace and champion the cause of white supremacy. He became a servant of the enemy, while believing that he was doing the will of God and soliciting His help in his endeavors.

I was shocked and saddened by what I had discovered—shocked because I never imagined him to be anything other than what I had always known of him via the media and saddened because I did not know the whole story and had judged him unfairly. I did not excuse his behavior or what he had done (and is still doing), but now I knew and understood the reason for (and the spirit behind) his behavior and motives. I was also angry that the enemy had taken advantage of someone with gifts, skills, and abilities given to him by God for a specific calling and used those gifts and abilities to hurt others. The Holy Spirit told me that David Duke could be another Paul. I knew in my spirit that he had been called to the ministry. God had a work for David Duke—a work for good, not for evil and for *all* people, not just white people.

As my research and note-taking concluded, I found myself praying fervently for this man, and for the wisdom, courage, and clarity of thought and mind to write this important letter as instructed by the Holy Spirit. As always, God was faithful. Eleven days later, His message to David Duke was completed and mailed on Monday, July 10, 2000. I never received a response, nor was the letter returned. What I do know was that the anointing was upon me and attended the communication. That morning, I had a sense of urgency in my spirit that the letter had to be mailed *that day*. Once the letter was finished and printed, I hurried to the post office, arriving fifteen minutes before closing. After paying the postage at the counter and accepting my receipt from the clerk, I left the building. The moment I stepped outside, the anointing finally lifted. While I was happy about the conclusion of my task, the enemy was not, and he made his displeasure known in a supernatural manner.

Two days later, flies mysteriously began invading our home. Their appearances were confined mainly to the kitchen and dining room areas. Ordinarily, I would have thought nothing of it since flies come in when one of the doors is opened. This was different. A family friend had come by the house to visit, and he and my father were commenting on—as well as baffled by—the numerous flies. They could not understand from where the flies were coming. I knew what was going on but remained silent. This was spiritual warfare in manifestation. Additionally, the fact that I killed several flies with the fly swatter, only to see them *literally multiply* before my eyes, was indicative of a demonic attack. My mother suspected the same thing but did not know the cause for it. I knew I would have to say something, lest something worse occurred. Without divulging any details about the letter or the recipient's identity, I told her briefly in private that I had written a letter to a prominent politician. The flies were Satan's method of intimidation. My mother agreed. We then took authority over the demonic forces in operation and bound them in the name of Jesus. The next day, when I had the house to myself, I used that opportunity to anoint the entire house (inside and outside) with oil. Afterward, I prayed and asked the Father to cover and seal our home with the blood of Jesus. Within two days, the flies were gone.

Second Corinthians 13:1 says, "In the mouth of two or three witnesses shall every word be established." The flies were a witness as well as a sign that my obedience to God had impacted the spirit world and incurred the wrath of Satan. I was soon to acquire two more "witnesses."

The second witness came shortly after mailing the letter to Mr. Duke. The following Saturday night, I was channel surfing and happened to turn to TBN. Christian recording artist Carmen was hosting his own television program at the time. I was about to change the channel when my hand was stayed on the remote control. At that precise moment, a clip was being shown of a man giving his testimony of becoming a born again Christian. He had been an Imperial Wizard in the local Ku Klux Klan in his area, was twice divorced, had problems with alcohol, and was on the verge of committing suicide. As he contemplated taking his own life (he had a handgun resting on his lap), his eyes fell upon a Bible lying on a nearby table. He felt impressed to pick it up. It fell open to Galatians 3, and verse 28 caught his eyes: "There is neither Jew nor Greek, there is neither bond nor free, there is neither male nor female: *for ye are all one in Christ Jesus.*" He was convicted by the Holy Spirit and born again that night. Instead of ending his life, he received eternal life by asking Jesus to forgive him of his sins and come into his heart, and accepting Him as his personal Savior and Lord.

Next, he called a local black minister, whom he had been repeatedly harassing, to make amends, even calling him "brother." The two eventually became friends and began working on various projects together in an effort to foster good relationships in their community. Their personal relationship and community involvement garnered the attention of the media, and their story was featured in their local newspaper.

When the segment concluded, Carmen then introduced his guest, Ben Kinchlow. The topic of discussion centered on race relations. At one point, Carmen asked Ben what he thought was the reason for the racial problems, especially in America. Ben's response consisted of one word: *sin*! I nearly fell off the couch! His reply was *exactly* what the Holy Spirit revealed to me and told me to include in the letter to Mr. Duke! Carmen's inquiry to Ben was the same as my inquiry to the Father. It was through praying in tongues that the Holy Spirit revealed to me what the real cause of racial discord (or any type of discord) is: *sin*.

The final witness occurred sometime later. One day, quite

unexpectedly, the Holy Spirit flashed something into my mind that I had not thought about in approximately thirty years. The memory of it startled me. I never imagined that something that happened when I was twelve years old would prepare me for what I would experience many years later.

The "something" the Holy Spirit brought to my remembrance was an article that had appeared in our local newspaper. It was about a man who had once held a high position in the Ku Klux Klan and had become a born again Christian. Not only was he born again, he was also a minister or priest. Along with the article was a picture of the man. The specifics concerning his physical features are a blur. I do recall him wearing a black clerical outfit with a high white neck collar; a chain with a large cross that adorned his neck; and dark hair with a receding hairline. His name and the contents of the article have long since been forgotten. But even at the age of twelve, I remember being surprised, if not incredulous, that a former Klansman was no longer advocating hatred, but preaching the gospel. Somehow, it seemed so strange, even impossible, to believe that a Klansman could really change. I don't know why I thought or felt that way, but I did. Then again, I was still a child and seeing things from a child's point of view. I thank the Lord for helping me to see things differently—from His point of view.

These "witnesses" attest to the truth that "the kingdom of God is not in word [or in word only], but in power" (1 Corinthians 4:20). The men in both cases are testimonies that the power of the gospel and the Holy Spirit can transform commonplace sinners into citizens of the kingdom of God.

In the next chapter, I will share with you excerpts from the letter written to David Duke. It will not only provide background information, but a foundation upon which understanding and unity can be initiated and fostered. Once these truths as revealed by the Holy Spirit are read and internalized, the plan and purpose God envisioned of oneness among the believers in the body of Christ will be realized.

Chapter 7

A Letter to a Former Klansman

To open their eyes, and to turn them from darkness to light, and from the power of Satan unto God, that they may receive forgiveness of sins, and inheritance among them which are sanctified by faith that is in me.

—Acts 26:18

July 10, 2000

Dear Mr. Duke:

I welcome this opportunity to write to you, although the thought of doing so never entered my mind ... until now. Indeed, I can give no reasonable explanation for writing other than the fact that I am strongly impressed by the Spirit of God to do so.

As a Christian, I have an obligation and a spiritual responsibility to share with you what the Holy Spirit has revealed to me. While I anticipate that you may not/will not concur with the views expressed in this communication, it is my prayer that you will be willing to give thoughtful consideration to this discourse, and receive these words in the spirit in which they are written.

My Awakening: A Spiritual Experience

Recently, I had an opportunity to read excerpts from your book entitled *My Awakening: A Path to Racial Understanding.* While I did not concur with some of the views/statements presented, what I read was interesting and informative.

I have also experienced an awakening, one that has taken me down a rough and often emotional path to racial understanding. I, too, was in search of the truth regarding the matter of race. I read numerous books, magazines, and newspaper articles on the subject, and viewed documentaries and movies via television and videos. They left me enlightened, but ambivalent, and with more questions than answers. It was frustrating. But ... truth began to stir my spirit little by little. My awakening was the result of *revelation*, not education, "For I neither received it of man, neither was I taught it, but by the revelation of Jesus Christ" (Galatians 1.12).

It is understandable as to why you would employ the use of historical documentation in presenting your views. One generally cannot dispute what is fact and what lends credence to one's beliefs. Nor do I dispute the relevancy of history, science, etc., provided they are viewed in their proper perspective. To use various fields of study, however, to justify or validate that one race is superior to another is without merit, no matter how overwhelming the evidence is to the contrary. I am no more responsible for being the race, color, and sex that I am any more than you are responsible for being the race, color, and sex that you are. I did not ask to be a black woman, nor did you choose to be a white man. But these aspects and features of our persons were determined before the foundation of the world.

Wisdom: The Pearl of Great Price

In searching for truth on any given subject, it is important to remember that knowledge and wisdom produce understanding. Knowledge ... is merely a compilation of facts. Wisdom is needed in order to apply the knowledge acquired in an appropriate manner in any given situation. In other words, *wisdom is the right use of knowledge*. There is *human wisdom*, by which most of us are influenced and governed, and then there is *true wisdom*, which comes from God. "For the LORD giveth wisdom: out of his mouth cometh knowledge and understanding" (Proverbs 2:6).

In 1 Kings 3:5–14, the LORD appeared to King Solomon in a dream at night in Gibeon, and asked Solomon what he desired Him to do for him. Solomon's request was for the LORD to give him "an understanding heart", a heart that listens or hears, that he might rightly judge God's people. The LORD honored Solomon's request and told him that He would also give him that for which he had not asked: riches and honor. Additionally, if Solomon was obedient in following the LORD, his life would be prolonged. There had never been, nor would there ever be another king like Solomon. Do you know why Solomon was wise? He was wise because he was humble enough to recognize and acknowledge his limitations. He was young and inexperienced; he didn't know everything. That's why God could answer his request. Later on in his life, Solomon transgressed the commandments of God by becoming involved in idolatry as a result of the many women he married. Eventually, he repented of his sins and returned to the LORD. But it was his request at the beginning of his reign for an understanding heart that enabled him to be a successful and wise king.

I emphasized the importance of wisdom to show that *knowledge without wisdom is dangerous*! One can have convictions and beliefs for years, only to discover later on that the premise for those beliefs was based on information that proved to be partially true or was totally false. The danger is that when truth is actually revealed, many are unwilling and/or unable to accept it. They have believed a lie for so long that it has become truth to them. Sadly, many do not wish to relinquish an idea or a belief that is familiar to or comfortable for them.

To fully understand the need for knowledge and wisdom

as it relates to racial conflicts, it is necessary to identify the underlying cause of the problem and its origin.

What's Sin Got to Do with It?

Sin made its first appearance before the world was created. Lucifer, now Satan, was a covering cherub in heaven and was next to Christ in terms of position. However, he was not happy with his position and was jealous of Christ ... so much so that he decided that he should occupy the position held by God the Father and incited a rebellion among some of the angels against Him. The rebellion led to war in heaven, and the result was that Satan and a third of the angelic host lost their first estate (see Isaiah 14:12–15; Revelation 12:7–9, 12).

When Satan and his angels were cast out of heaven, they eventually came to earth. Satan succeeded in deceiving Eve through the medium of a serpent. He told her that if she disobeyed God's command not to eat the fruit of the tree in the midst of the garden of Eden (the tree of knowledge of good and evil), she would not surely die and would be as a god herself. This suggestion appealed to Eve, and she ate some of the fruit. She convinced her husband, Adam, that the serpent must be right in what he had said. Adam was not deceived; he disobeyed because of his love for Eve. Like Satan, their disobedience caused them to lose their first estate, for they could no longer stay in their beautiful Eden home. Sin has its basis in pride and self; its end is ruin, degradation, and death (Romans 6:23). The results of that one act of disobedience have perpetuated into the chaos and unrest that now exist.

The Truth of the Matter in Black and White

Satan used the forbidden fruit as a smokescreen to conceal his true purpose: to destroy our first parents, Adam and Eve. He desired to incite them to disobey the just commands of God and incur upon themselves (and the human race) the guilt and penalty of sin as he and his host had done. *Satan's tactics never change, but the smokescreens do*, depending on the situation. The underlying cause of the world's problems is *sin*! Satan's sole purpose is to keep the minds of the masses engaged in and with temporal distractions and issues so they will be unable to discern his motives and methods. He does not want them to have an opportunity to hear the gospel of Jesus Christ (let alone accept it) that they might be saved, receive forgiveness for their sins, and walk in newness of life. "But if our gospel be hid, it is hid to them that are lost: In whom the god of this world (Satan) hath blinded the minds of them which believe not, lest the light of the glorious gospel of Christ, who is the image of God, should shine unto them" (2 Corinthians 4:3–4). Satan wants people to die in their sins and receive the punishment that awaits him and his evil host, along with all who have rejected God's message of love and mercy.

There are various organizations, under the guise of advocating civil rights, who are endeavoring to effect changes in our society using means and methods at their disposal to accomplish their goals and purposes via legislation, violence, threats/manipulation, marches, protests, the Internet, etc. Such efforts, however, will not change a stubborn will or a stubborn heart hardened by hatred and/or ignorance and unbelief. *There is no natural solution for a spiritual problem*! What many people do not realize or believe, including many professed Christians, is that we are involved in a *spiritual warfare*. "For we are not wrestling with flesh and blood [contending only with physical opponents], but against the despotisms, against the powers, against [the master spirits who are] the world rulers of this present darkness, against the spirit forces of wickedness in the heavenly (supernatural) sphere" (Ephesians 6:12, AMP). There is a double kingdom in operation: a *natural* kingdom (visible) and a *spiritual* kingdom (invisible), *and the latter controls the former*. As a result, there are demonic strongholds in force in every city and nation. Satan uses individuals and groups to divide and conquer.

The tensions and strife that currently exist in our world attest to Satan's success in this regard.

On the other hand, God's will is to reconcile the world to Himself through His Son. He desires that we, His followers, be one, even as He and the Son are one. God loves each of us as if there was not another person on the earth. He is not willing that *any* should perish, but that *all* should come to repentance and the knowledge of the truth.

The Conclusion of the Whole Matter

Mr. Duke, you possess certain traits of character that I deem admirable in any person. You are knowledgeable, well read, a deep thinker, zealous, organized, steadfast in adversity, and passionate. You are an author and a lecturer and have traveled extensively. God has gifted you with leadership qualities and abilities that you might do a great work for Him. God has a wonderful plan for your life, but you will never know what it is unless you give Him an opportunity to reveal it to you. You have accomplished much in your lifetime; but "Except the LORD build the house, they labour in vain that build it" (Psalm 127:1). If what is done is of one's own devising, it will surely come to nothing (John 6:63). God's Word and His work will be forthcoming, and no amount of fury and/or opposition shall overthrow what He has ordained to be accomplished in the earth.

It has been said that one man can affect the many. It was one man's book that changed the course of your life. One man's book was responsible for your becoming the man that you are today. My prayer is that you will permit another Man to again change the course of your life and make you a blessing to *all* people.

Respectfully,

Evangeline Henderson

Epilogue

Behold, how good and how pleasant it is for brethren to dwell together in unity!

—Psalm 133:1

God created man to be a social being. Man was not only to have a relationship with God but also with others. All of us are different in terms of background, culture, intellectual abilities, educational privileges, and spiritual progress. Nevertheless, we are to put aside our differences, put the interests of others above our own, and share our gifts, talents, and abilities with others so the final outcome will be such that, working together in unity, we will accomplish the work that God has given us to do.

In 1 Corinthians 12:12–27, we have a perfect example of how the body of Christ should function by comparing it with the physical body. The physical body is comprised of various organs, cells, and other body parts as well as a head. Some parts are visible, while other components are hidden. Some have a major role, others a lesser role. *No one part can perform all the functions of the body or act independently of the others. Every part of the body has its specific assignment in the body, but is effective only as it works in conjunction with the other parts.* All the parts, though diverse, working together, cause the body to function in a normal manner. When one part is not at full capacity or does not function at all, the whole body suffers. The same principle applies to people in general, and the body of Christ in particular.

Whether we like it or not, we need one another in order to function individually and corporately.

We will never agree on everything. The twelve disciples were constantly arguing about who among them was the greatest (Matthew 20:20–24; Mark 9:33–35). Murmurings arose from the Greek Jews against the Hebrews because their widows were neglected in the daily distribution of food and assistance (Acts 6:1–6). Paul and Barnabas had a heated verbal confrontation concerning John Mark and ended up separating, each choosing a different co-laborer (Acts 15:36–41). Paul's attitude and feelings toward John Mark later changed as he deemed him profitable to him for the ministry (2 Timothy 4:11).

As we study the Word of God, solicit the help of the Holy Spirit, and function in our respective ministry and spiritual gifts, we will exhibit the fruit of the Spirit and come into the unity of the faith (Galatians 5:22–23; Ephesians 4:13). When the character of Christ has been genuinely manifested in the life of those who hear and heed His voice, "And this gospel of the kingdom shall be preached in all the world for a witness unto all nations ... then shall the end come" (Matthew 24:14).

The sources of our oppression—Satan, sin, and sinners—will finally be destroyed. The former things in this life that have made our existence here on earth miserable, including racism, will be permanently deleted from our memories. I'm looking forward to that day. What about you?

When Jesus returns to gather His children, what a day of rejoicing that will be! Hallelujah! Finally, we will all be one!

The Sinner's Prayer to Receive Salvation

The most important decision that you will ever make will involve the salvation of your soul and where you will spend eternity. If you would like to receive Jesus as your personal Savior and Lord, I invite you to pray this prayer:

Dear Heavenly Father:

I come to you in the name of Your Son, Jesus. According to Your Word, if the wicked forsake his way, and the unrighteous man his thoughts, and returns to You, You will have mercy upon him, and he will be abundantly pardoned (Isaiah 55:7). I ask You to be merciful to me, a sinner, and forgive me of all my sins (Luke 18:13; 1 John 1:9).

Romans 10:9–10 says "That if thou shalt confess with thy mouth the Lord Jesus, and shalt believe in thine heart that God hath raised him from the dead, thou shalt be saved. For with the heart man believeth unto righteousness; and with the mouth confession is made unto salvation." I confess with my mouth that Jesus is the Son of God. I believe in my heart that God raised Him from the dead. Jesus is now the Lord of my life, and by faith, I am saved! Thank You, Father, in Jesus's name. Amen.

If you prayed this prayer, you just became a born again Christian, a new creation in Christ (2 Corinthians 5:17). Welcome to the family of God! Find a good Bible-based church where the uncompromised Word of God is being preached and taught, and the anointing of God destroys the yoke of bondage (Isaiah 10:27).

Prayer to Receive the Baptism of the Holy Spirit

Jesus taught that there is a subsequent experience to salvation: the baptism of the Holy Spirit (John 7:37–39; Acts 2:1–4).

On the day of Pentecost, as Peter preached to the Jews gathered in Jerusalem, he said to them, "Repent, and be baptized every one of you in the name of Jesus Christ for the remission of sins, and *ye shall receive the gift of the Holy Ghost. For the promise is unto you, and to your children, and to all that are afar off, even as many as the Lord our God shall call*" (Acts 2:38–39).

If you wish to receive the promise of the Holy Spirit that will be a blessing to you, your family, the body of Christ, and the world, simply pray the following prayer:

Heavenly Father:

I come to you in the name of Jesus. Jesus said that You are more willing to give the Holy Spirit to them that ask You than earthly parents are to give good gifts to their children (Luke 11:13).

Father, I ask You to fill me with Your Holy Spirit. By faith, I believe I receive Him now with the evidence of speaking in other tongues. Thank You in Jesus's name. Amen.

When you have concluded your prayer, exercise your faith by opening your mouth, and speaking out the supernatural language that the Holy Spirit gives you. Don't try to *think* about what you are saying or trying to say. *Allow the Holy Spirit to give you the utterance* (Acts 2:4).

As you continually speak in tongues, you will begin to grow spiritually and become more spiritually enlightened, and your faith will be stimulated and strengthened. Speaking in other tongues is also the doorway that leads to the operation and manifestation of the gifts of the Spirit (as the Spirit wills) in your personal life and ministry.

For more information on receiving the Holy Spirit and spiritual gifts, I recommend the following resources by Kenneth E. Hagin:

- *Baptism in the Holy Spirit (Study Guide)*
- *Gifts of the Holy Spirit (Study Guide)*
- *Why Tongues? (Minibook)*
- *Tongues: Their Scriptural Purpose (three-CD series)*
- *Tongues: Beyond the Upper Room (Book)*

You may obtain these resources by accessing one or more of the following:

- Any Christian bookstore
- Website: www.rhema.org/store
- Write to: Kenneth Hagin Ministries, P.O. Box 50126, Tulsa, OK 74150-0126

Another excellent reference on the subject of tongues is *The Walk of the Spirit—The Walk of Power: The Vital Role of Praying in Tongues* by Dave Roberson. For information concerning a copy of his book or about Pastor Roberson's ministry, you may call or write to:

Dave Roberson Ministries
The Family Prayer Center
P.O. Box 725
Tulsa, OK 74101-9657
U. S. A.
Phone: (918) 298-7729 (Monday—Thursday, 9:00 a. m. – 4:00
    p. m., CT)
Fax: (918) 299-0464
Website: www.daveroberson.org

Printed in the United States
By Bookmasters